A gift for your classroom
From Peterson PTA
2008~2009

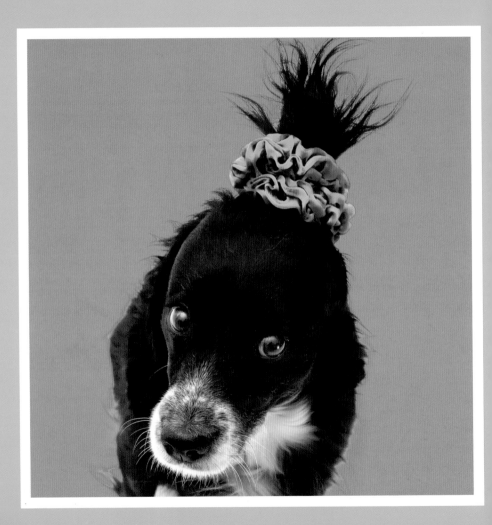

BAD FUR DAYS

By Gabrielle Tolliver

RUNNING PRESS
PHILADELPHIA · LONDON

© 2008 by Gabrielle Tolliver
All rights reserved under the Pan-American and International Copyright Conventions
Printed in China

This book may not be reproduced in whole or in part, in any form or by any means, electronic or mechanical, including photocopying, recording, or by any information storage and retrieval system now known or hereafter invented, without written permission from the publisher.

9 8 7 6 5 4 3 2 1
Digit on the right indicates the number of this printing

Library of Congress Control Number: 2007937300

ISBN 978-0-7624-3544-9

Cover and interior design by Corinda Cook
Edited by Greg Jones
Typography: Antique Olive, Arial, Avenir, Caslon, Clarendon, Baileywick, Bank Gothic, Bodoni, Bordeaux, Bossa Nova, Calaban, Chicken Basket, Chowderhead, Congo, Copperplate, Dairyland, Dorchester Script, Ed, Goudy, Monotype Sorts, Optima, Rockwell, Runic, Sassoon, Stone Sans, TF Roux Borders, Tiki, Trade Gothic, and Typography of Coop

Running Press Book Publishers
2300 Chestnut Street
Philadelphia, Pennsylvania 19103-4371

Visit us on the web!
www.runningpress.com

WARNING: This book comes with a P-XXX rating, which means under no circumstance should you show it to your pet. The images of fur-do failure on the pages that follow are too extreme for safe viewing by sensitive animals. We strongly advise that you keep your copy of *Bad Fur Days* under lock and key and only take it out while your pet is napping or out in the yard chasing grasshoppers.

And, please, if you find that you dislike this book, resist the urge to tear out its pages and use them to line the litter box or dog cage. One glimpse of a photo—even a picture partially covered by cat litter or dog dirt—could cause your pet weeks of recurring nightmares and restless sleep. All that tossing and turning in bed would ensure that your pet endures many subsequent bad fur days. It might even lead to him or her ending up in the sequel. You have been advised.

YOU THINK YOU SUFFER THROUGH BAD HAIR DAYS?

Picture the case of "bed head" you'd wake up with each morning if you spent 18-hours-a-day in bed, like your typical feline does.

Imagine how often your 'do would come undone if you stuck your head out the window of a fast-moving car, the way your average dog does every chance he gets.

Or envision the daily dilemma faced by the offspring of a sleek dalmatian father and a longhaired Irish setter mother—with no access to a trimmer or color-correction products.

Just reading about it is probably enough to make your hair stand up on the back of your neck. (Or your fur, if you're a critter whose master didn't heed the warning above.) It should also help you appreciate why animals endure so many bad fur days. Not to mention a whole lot of bad feather, wool, mane, quill, and fin days. And let's not even get into all the social, emotional, professional, and dating disadvantages that a laughable lid brings with it.

8

Bad Fur Days celebrates these court jesters of the animal kingdom as they bravely battle bad fur-dos, fleas, shedding, bubble baths, fashion flubs, catastrophic coat markings, and all the accompanying woes. In the pages that follow, you'll find cats, dogs, llamas, birds, goats, rabbits, horses, simians and other animals coping with a coiffure crisis that would probably drive most humans to hide their heads beneath a baseball hat. Or a motorcycle helmet. Or under their bedspreads until they could arrange for an emergency house call from a hairstylist.

So give your love as well as your laughter for these courageous and hilarious critters. All animals deserve our kindness and respect—plus, when necessary, a quick brushing disguised as affectionate petting to straighten out their unfortunate 'dos and help them get through those bad fur days.

Devon realizes that she's overdone it again with the volumizing conditioner.

Ralph and Emma compare early morning cases of riverbed head.

As his scarf falls
off his face,
Monty is revealed
as the infamous
baby bottle bandit.

"Maybe my wife is right—it's time for an extreme makeover."

The three finalists in the Equine Fabio Lookalike Contest vogue one last time for the judges.

Phyllis wonders if today is the day the '70s megafro finally comes back into vogue.

Shaun Cassidy tries to come to grips with his reincarnation.

"Lend me a talon, would you, Bert? My landing gear is stuck open again."

Way behind her wool growth,
Gina wonders if she
should pick up a faux fur coat
for the coming winter.

After yet another toddler
mistakes her for cotton
candy, Candice begs
her master to take her
home from the circus.

SICK OF DOING CRUNCHES, LOU WONDERS IF HE CAN GET HIS STYLIST TO CORNROW A SIX-PACK AB PATTERN INTO HIS BELLY FUR.

Helen senses that her husband Harold is lying about how much he likes her new chartreuse highlights.

With the black spot on his nose not responding to acne creams, Todd decides to consult a furmatologist.

Claude decides it's time to have a word with his master about static cling.

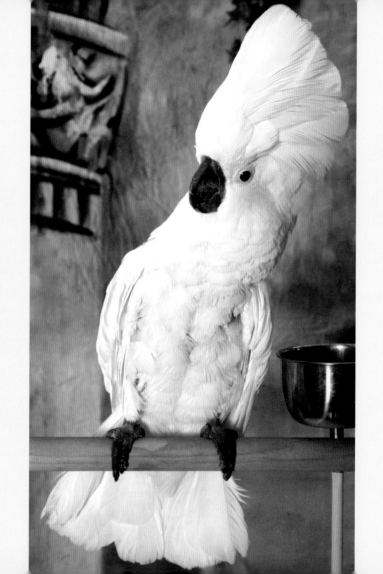

Trevor confesses to his analyst that he believes he's the second coming of King Tut.

Gary ruins the family portrait by hacking up a furball.

43

Some days, no matter what you try, you just can't get your ear-do to work.

Tiffany takes a swing at Heather over her "blondes have more fleas" snipe.

After breaking an average of six combs per week in his quills, Woody goes with a buzz cut.

When all the prescription
powders and shampoos fail,
Martin turns to voodoo
to clear up his flea problem.

"He's really overdoing it with his macho plumage flexing this spring."

53

Timmy tries to scare off the neighborhood tomcat by pretending he's turning into a miniature werewolf.

As Aunt Betty lowers
her giant rear toward him,
Fluffy realizes his
fur coloring makes him
nearly invisible on
the new Persian couch.

Howard wonders if it's too late to cash in his money-back guarantee from Fur Club for Simians.

Louise hopes donkey designers soon replace "twig chic" with a more comfortable style of outerwear.

Kim displays the ill effects of getting only 14 hours of sleep per night instead of the recommended 19.

Even after an hour
of combing, blow-drying,
and moussing,
Bill still can't tease
his fur out of its
unflattering middle part.

"I coulda' been a Kentucky Derby contender . . . if I coulda' seen my way into the starting gate."

With all the catnip gone,
Tony tries to liven up the party
with his imitation of Italy.

Billy decides to give up trying to stay in shape with yoga and just go back to chasing cars and mailmen.

**Barton begins
to regret
appearing as a
guest star
on *Serengati Ink*.**

Sticking his head out of the window for the entire cross-country roadtrip fails to clear up Brock's dandruff.

Tina digests the news that *Vogue* just put cheetah skin on its Spring "out" list.

Leona feels much better since kicking her botox addiction, but looks so much worse.

Gwendolyn's innovative punk look nets her "Worst of Show" from the Westminster judges.

Craig cements his status as
the black sheep of the family
by graffiti tagging
his mother and little sister.

PETRA TWISTS HER BODY INTO AN "F" TO BEGIN SPELLING OUT "F-O-O-D" TO LET HER MASTER KNOW THAT SHE'S WAY OVERDUE FOR LUNCH.

"For the last time: it's a birthmark, not a bull's eye."

Reggie can't believe he let the

pushy salesman talk

him into installing fur siding

on his kitty condo.

89

TERRY GOES ON THE LAM UNTIL HER DISASTROUS SPIRAL PERM GROWS OUT.

Weary of all the primping required on the dog-show circuit, Jillian plots a move into the lapdog racket.

JABBA
THE
MUTT

94

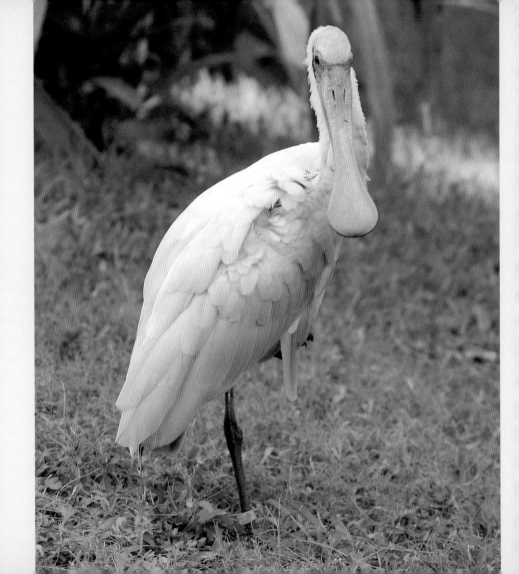

Dwayne endures another round of lawn-ornament jokes from a group of rowdy bird watchers.

Trudi waits for her Brazilian Fur Straightening Treatment to wear off so she can fit her head back through the fence.

Heavy metal trio Steel Wool trudge home after failing to impress the judges at the County Fair Talent Show.

Rita storms off the set of the marine life documentary after the producers fail to meet her demands for a personal shell stylist.

Brenda decides to stop fighting the black-cat stigma and just go with it.

The B Street Bloodshots let the Lhasa Apso know what they think of fancy, long-haired breeds coming onto their turf.

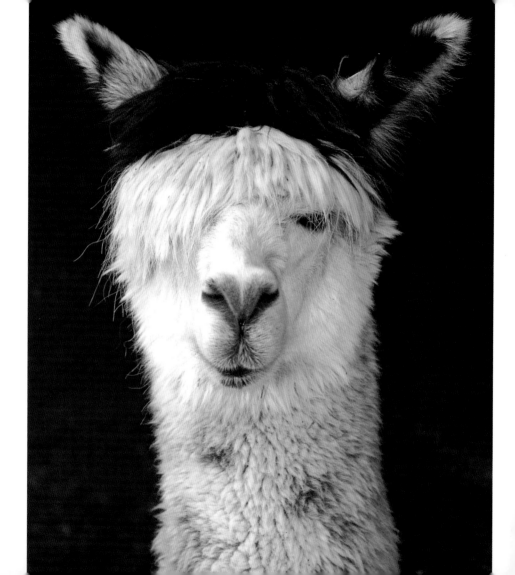

Serge isn't fooling
anyone with
his new $5 toupee.

Mutt underdog Rocky Alpoa feels the sweat dripping down his fur as he arrives for his Frisbee Fetch title bout vs. longtime champ Apollo Pure Breed.

Former mob racehorse Wisey Jones tries to blend with the Wyoming cow herd he was placed into by the Federal Witness Protection Program.

Millie begins to suspect
that there's a catch
to Rancher Dan's
free shape-and-trim offer.

After receiving nothing but laughing emoticons in response to his online personal ad, Ezekiel considers updating his look from Classic Amish.

Realizing her ponytail
is way passé,
Ginger wonders if she
should re-style
her mane into a bob.

Heddy worries that her pink furlights and jacket are too matchy-matchy.

"One more
Pepe Le Pew
crack, and
I'll headbutt
you in
the shins."

Sue realizes her stylist took her request for a "wedge cut" a little too literally.

IAN PERFORMS AT THE LOCAL KARAOKE BAR, TRYING TO RECAPTURE HIS GLORY DAYS IN THE 1980s BIG PLUMAGE BAND, A FLOCK OF PARROTS.

Butch vows to never again complain that the wind feels a little chilly on his bare fur.

EVEN WITH HIS NEW PAULIE WALNUTS HIGHLIGHTS, VITO CAN'T GAIN ENTRY INTO LA COSA NESTRA CRIME FLOCK.

Mildred serves as a cautionary tale on the hazards of cutting your own bangs.

LEGENDARY FUR STYLIST VIDAL BABOON LAMENTS THE CANNIBALISM OUTBREAK CAUSED BY HIS NEW BANANA-SCENTED SHAMPOO FOR SIMIANS.

As he spots his mistress's foot
coming toward him,
Biff realizes that he's been
mistaken for a bedroom slipper.

JEFF IS CRUSHED TO FIND OUT THAT HE'S ADOPTED.

With dismal reviews and record-low ratings, *Magnum B.I.: Lost Easter Egg Detective* gets canceled after only one episode.

AFTER CATCHING HER REFLECTION IN THE POND, SHIRLEY CONCLUDES IT'S TIME TO SPLURGE ON A NEW PERM AND BEAK JOB.

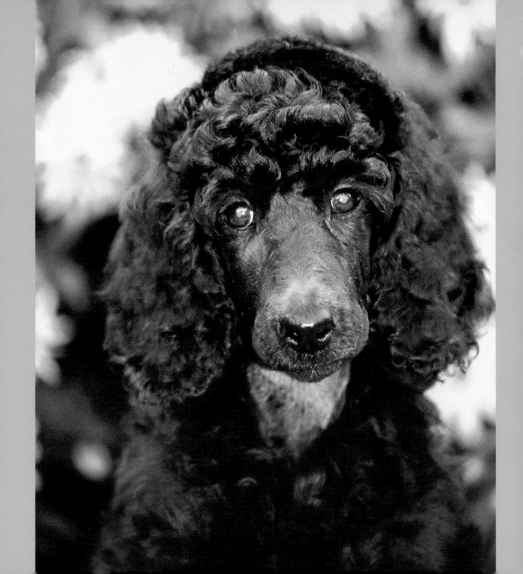

Jake loses his street cred, watchdog job, and girlfriend within hours of unveiling his new jeri-curl perm.

Hank wonders if he has the right coloring to pull off his bird-hunting strategy of disguising himself as a weather vane.

Gil's ambitious scheme to ambush the Easter Bunny nets only a marshmallow mouse melted onto his fur.

Lily stares down the electrical outlet that just re-did her 'do.

Reginald dreams about turning into a giant storm cloud to circle the globe, raining on parades, picnics, and outdoor dog shows.

MORGAN CONNORS, PRESIDENT OF THE PRINCESS LEIA FAN CLUB FOR LEMURS.

Fifi has to laugh to keep from crying about her new mullet.

Hearing that horizontal stripes add 15 pounds to your rump, Shannon gallops to the mall to buy a pair of jeans.